The Journey Back To You

IT'S WORTH THE TRIP

Lakisha Selby

The Journey Back to You
It's Worth the Trip
Copyright, @2019 Lakisha Selby

Printed in the United States of America
First Printing, 2019
ISBN 978-0-692-08378-9
Cover Designer: Sarah Cook

DEDICATION

I would like to thank God for allowing me to continue my journey to see my vision come to pass. Without God on my side, I don't know where I would be. There were some things that should have killed me. However, He allowed me to survive every challenge, circumstance, obstacle, and situation that came my way. For that I am thankful.

"For I know the plans I have for you," declares the LORD, "plans to prosper you and not to harm you, plans to give you hope and a future."
-Jeremiah 29:11

I dedicate this book to my children Darion, Diamond, Deionna and Dwayne Jr. I love you with all my heart. You keep me young and living. I want you to know that you can do anything through Christ that strengthens you. Remember to always LEAD and never FOLLOW.

ACKNOWLEDGEMENTS

To my angels in Heaven, continue to watch over me. I love you.

To my father in Heaven, *John Wing*, I miss you saying, "Girl go home and mind your business." I love you and thanks for being the best father a girl could ever ask for. I think I may have gotten my mouth from you. You were never afraid to speak what was on your mind.

To my mother *Jacqueline Wing* who supports me in everything that I do. I love you. Your dream has come true. I remember you saying that you had a dream I was speaking to hundreds of women in one room. Won't He do it?

To my siblings *Jonnise* & *Tiffany*, what would you do without me? I love you! It has not always been easy having an older sibling such as me; however I hope I've been a great role model for you.

To my niece and nephews, I love you. I would not trade you for the world.

To my girlfriends that have turned into my sisters. Thank you for being a listening ear for all my early/late phone calls. I love you gals. Through the disagreements to the agreements, I am grateful to have some wonderful women in my life.

To my family and friends, I love you and thank you for all your support.

To my spiritual leaders, *Pastor Shannon & Lady Nikki McNeil.* I thank you for every encouraging word that you have ever spoken into my life through every chapter. The good and the bad. Your words of encouragement and wisdom have helped me tremendously as I mature in my spiritual walk.

To everyone that has helped me through my journey whether good or bad, thank you. What the enemy meant for evil, God turned it around for my good.

To *Women Of Courage, Inc. & Young Ladies Of Courage,* you give me life and I run to you when I need to visit my happy place.

"Write the vision, and make it plain upon tables, that he may run that readeth it. For the vision is yet for an appointed time, but at the end it shall speak, and not lie: though it tarry, wait for it; because it will surely come, it will not tarry." -Habakkuk 2 2-3

CONTENTS

INTRODUCTION

This book was birthed through self-acceptance. When I look back over my life, I realized that there were people and things that were out of my control, that I could not change. I also knew that I didn't want to live in the past any longer, so I had to start examining my own life and accepting reality for what it really was. As much as I wanted to blame everyone for my problems and the reasons for my life not turning out the way that I thought it should have turned out, I had to accept responsibility for the part that I played in my own life. I decided that I had to move forward and stop looking backwards, it was time to head into a new direction.

It was no longer time to concern myself with what people thought about me or what they knew. I could no longer live for everybody else. I had to begin living for me. In 2018, I decided that I was going to begin my journey back to me. There were some things that I had to deal with within and there were some people I had to forgive.

It may sound selfish to some, but it's not selfish when you begin putting you first. As I began my journey, I wanted to help others begin theirs.

Your journey will not be easy, but it will be worth it. There is nothing in life that is easy. There will be some distractions, bumps in the road, and doubt, but you must remember that the journey you are about to travel is for you. As you decide to move on with your life, you will be motivated to go, then there will be times that you may slow down, and you may even stop during your journey and find yourself going backwards after you made up your mind you wanted to move forward.

Whether you slow down, stop or go back, remember you cannot quit! This journey is about you and you are worth it. No matter how many times you must start over, you will make it to your destination.

I utilize spiritual and natural principles in this book that have helped and continue to help me. Your spiritual and natural principles may be different than mine, however, use what will help you through your journey. I hope that this book will educate, empower and inspire you to become self-aware and accept things for what they were and accept things for what they will become.

Self-awareness: an awareness of one's own personality or individuality

__Self-acceptance__: the act or state of accepting oneself: the act or state of understanding and recognizing one's own abilities and limitations.

CHAPTER 1

JOURNEY

Journey: an act of traveling from one place to another; a long and often difficult process of personal change and development.

Have you ever been on a journey? Could you have made some better choices or decisions in your life that could have resulted in a better outcome? Have you taken responsibility for any of it? Would you like to start a journey to get to a place that you never thought you would get to? This is something to think about as you prepare yourself. This journey is about you, so why not start by analyzing yourself today. Your journey is not the same as mine, and my journey is not yours, but if we continue on this path, we may make it to our destination.

> **"If you don't go after what you want, you'll never have it. If you don't ask, the answer is always no. If you don't step forward, you're always in the same place" -Nora Roberts**

Accountability: the fact or condition of being accountable; responsibility.

Responsibility: the state or fact of being accountable or to blame for something.

CHAPTER 2

GETTING TO KNOW YOURSELF

---～---

> "Knowing yourself is the beginning of all wisdom." -Aristotle

Let's see how well you know yourself by answering the questions below. It's time to be honest with you. If you cannot relate to the question, leave it blank.

On a scale of 1 to 10, with 1 being, "not at all," and 10, "very." How well do you know yourself _____?

Who are you?

_____

_____

_____

_____

_____

What are your short-term goals?

_____

_____

_____

_____

_____

_____

What are your long-term goals?

_____

_____

_____

_____

_____

_____

Where are you in your life right now?

_____

_____

_____

_____

_____

_____

Are you where you would like to be in your career? Financially, personally and spiritually? If not, Why?

_____

_____

_____

_____

_____

How is your relationship with your children, parents, peers and siblings?

_____

_____

_____

_____

_____

If any, what could you improve in your relationship with your children, parents, peers and siblings?

_____

_____

_____

_____

_____

What do you like about yourself?

_____

_____

_____

_____

_____

_____

What don't you like about yourself?

_____

_____

_____

_____

_____

_____

What have you done in your life that you are proud of?

_____

_____

_____

_____

_____

_____

What legacy would you like to leave behind?

_____

_____

_____

_____

_____

How well do you manage your money? Could you improve your money management? If so how?

_____

_____

_____

_____

_____

If a relationship or job makes you unhappy, do you choose to stay or leave? Why?

_____

_____

_____

_____

_____

What do you fear about leaving your job or a bad relationship?

_____

_____

_____

_____

_____

If you have left a job or a bad relationship; what motivated you to leave?

_____

_____

_____

_____

_____

Who are the most important people in your life? Why?

_____

_____

_____

_____

_____

If you could change anything about yourself what would it be? Why?

_____

_____

_____

_____

_____

Why do you think it's important for you to get to know yourself?

_____

_____

_____

_____

_____

"It takes courage to grow up and
become who you really are."
-E.E. Cummings

The Journey Back To You

CHAPTER 3

IDENTITY

Identity: the distinguished character or personality of an individual

Let's move forward in this journey with understanding who you are. Whether you're applying for a job, school or anything that requires you to complete information about yourself, you're asked a series of questions. Those questions may consist of your name, age, gender, or race. I want you to sit down and think about who you really are. Do you know that you are more than how you self-identify yourself? It's okay that you may not fully know who you are.

Some people start off with knowing who they are or who they would like to become. Then there are others who grow into knowing who they are. However, something tragic could occur which could cause some to lose their identity. Are you identifying yourself based on the hurt, mistakes or people from your past? Be encouraged. You can get your identity back. Remember, it's okay to be different. So, let's get to practicing.

How I identify myself: I am Lakisha Selby. I am 39 years old. I am an African-American Christian female.

Remember we are all different and come from different backgrounds. We don't self-identify in the same way.

Now how do you identify yourself:

_____

_____

_____

_____

_____

Now that you have your identity, ask yourself, **"Who am I?** Look in the mirror and ask yourself again, **"Who am I? Are you identifying yourself by how others have identified you?** I remember looking in the mirror and asking myself, **"Who am I?** The first thing that I stated is I am beautiful! I have brown eyes! I like my hair! But I never answered the question, **"Who am I?** I was more than what I observed on the outside. However at that time that's what I thought identity was for me.

You are not what has happened to you. You may have experienced an abortion, abuse, (emotional or physical), bankruptcy, depression, divorce, death, incarceration, loss of employment, low self-esteem, financial difficulties, mental health, single parenting, or teen pregnancy. No matter, you are not your experience.

Experience: *practical contact with and observation of facts or events.*

If I was to ask myself today, "Who am I? I would say: My name is Lakisha Selby and I am not my experience. I am a Woman Of God. I am a Mother. I am a Daughter. I am a Sister. I am an Aunt. I am a Cousin. I am a Friend. I am a Woman Of Courage. I am a Survivor. I am Fearfully and Wonderfully Made. I am not perfect. I am Blessed. I am strong. I am beautiful. I am smart. I am loved. I am courageous! I am a leader. I am an author. I am an Entrepreneur. I am confident. I can do all things through Christ that strengthens me. I will change the world.

It wasn't until I began to build a relationship with God, change my mindset, change the way I spoke to myself and surrounded myself with like-minded individuals, that I became clearer about who I was. Even after this, I would find myself going back to the things and people that would have me second guessing who I was. Today I decided to continue my journey and focus not only on who I am, but also who I am becoming.

Remember you are different. I want you to write down who you are. Take a moment and ask yourself: "Who am I? Think about all the positive attributes that you possess and when those negative thoughts come to mind change them with positive thoughts.

I AM

_____

_____

_____

_____

_____

_____

_____

_____

You have now completed your I AM statements. Look in the mirror every day with a smile on your face and complete your I AM statements. Speak it **Boldly** and with **Confidence**.

Boldly: in a confident and courageous way, showing a willingness to take risks.

Confidence: the state of feeling certain about the truth of something; a feeling of self-assurance arising from one's appreciation of one's own abilities or qualities.

Now that you have identified who you are, you need a clear understanding of where you are going. Through this journey, you may get distracted or lose yourself along the way, but it will be your responsibility to go back and read your I AM statements and get back to your journey.

Where is it that you want to go?

_____
_____
_____
_____
_____
_____

As a young girl, I had my whole life mapped out. This was my life. I was going to get married and have two children, (a girl and boy), attend college to become a teacher and help the less fortunate. That was my dream. But what happens when things don't go the way you planned, and you must re-route?

Re-route: *to switch to a different route*

What challenges or obstacles did you experience in life that caused you to change directions, (ex: teen pregnancy, financial problems)?

_____

_____

_____

_____

_____

As I have stated above, I always wanted to be a mother. Well that did happen, however it happened when I least expected it to. At the age of 16, I became pregnant. I had my first child at the age of 17. My plan to attend college right after high school was over. Having my child caused my plans to change. I didn't have a plan B, when my plan A didn't go the way I thought it would. Remember no matter how good our plans are; we must be prepared for the unexpected. Reality is that we spend years, months and days planning and those plans can fall apart in seconds. If I knew then what I know now, my Plan B would have consisted of communicating my plans to my parents to create a plan on supporting me with my child so that I could attend college.

> **"Just because you make a good plan, doesn't mean that's what's going to happen."**
> **-Taylor Swift, singer and songwriter**

What was your dream?

_____

_____

_____

_____

What did you do when your plans did not turn out the way you thought they should have turned out?

_____

_____

_____

Did you have a Plan B? If so what was it?

_____

_____

_____

_____

Just because things don't go the way you planned, doesn't mean you stop going. As you continue your journey, you will see that a lot of things may not go the way you plan, however, you must keep traveling. If you stop traveling, you may never make it to your destination.

***Destination:** the place to which someone or something is going or being sent.*

CHAPTER 4

MOVE FORWARD

__Move__: to proceed toward a certain state or condition

__Forward__: moving, tending, or leading toward a position in front

__Backwards__: toward or into the past

As you begin your journey, you will need to decide whether you will move forward or stay stuck in the past. This decision can take a day, week, month, months or years. The decision you make may not be easy, but it will be worth it. While you're making your decision, I want you to think about a person living with the disease of addiction. I hear a lot of individuals in recovery state that they continue to use drugs because they thought they could obtain the same high from the very first time. So, they continue to chase the high. Trying to get the results they acquired the very first time. Let's stop here.

What or who is keeping you from moving forward? Why?

_____

_____

_____

_____

_____

What results are you obtaining when you go backwards or stay in your comfort zone?

_____

_____

_____

_____

_____

What or who are you going back to during your journey? Why?

_____

_____

_____

_____

_____

Are you expecting someone to change? Who? It could be more than one person. Remember to add you first because the change must start within and with you.

As you wait for someone to change, you may be waiting. The only person that you can change is you. Everyone is not ready to change. Some people believe that they are fine and never see anything wrong with themselves. The reason that you are beginning this journey is because you want to see change within. You no longer can focus on trying to change someone who has not acknowledged that there is something wrong with him/her. You be the change that you would like to see in somebody else. Remember this journey is about you.

It's time to focus on you, but you do have to understand what and who is keeping you from moving forward. People will continue to show you who they are, while you keep ignoring the signs and believing that the person will change. The person may very well change, but it won't be when you want them to change. A person must be ready for change. If you don't take the risk and come out of your comfort zone, you will never move forward. The same person you're waiting to change will move forward without you and begin a new journey with someone else.

It's your recovery time. It's your time to heal. You owe it to yourself.

Recovery: a return to a normal state of health mind, or strength; the action or process of regaining possession or control of something stolen or lost

Are you the person that is afraid of the unknown because you're so comfortable with living in the past?

Past: Gone by in time and no longer existing; having existed or taken place in a period before the present

I can remember being afraid of going over the Chesapeake Bay Bridge in Virginia. I was only afraid because I did not know what to expect. I had viewed pictures online and heard horrible stories about the bridge. I never had the chance to experience the bridge for myself because my mind was already made up from everybody else's viewpoint. Don't allow your decisions to be made based on someone else's experience. However, the Chesapeake Bay Bridge was not the only bridge that I was afraid of. To be honest I was afraid of all bridges.

Every time I went over a bridge, I would say to myself, "For God did not give me the spirit of fear, but of power, love and a sound mind." Before I knew it, my fear of bridges went all the way back to when I began traveling to Brooklyn, New York alone. Even when I had people in the car with me, they did not know that I was afraid of bridges. As you travel your journey, there may be some things that you have to keep to yourself, until you become **BOLD** and no longer operating in **FEAR**. Release your **FEARS** and replace them with **FAITH**.

Bold: *(of a person, action, or idea) showing an ability to take risks; confident and courageous.*

CHAPTER 5

FEAR

Fear: an unpleasant emotion caused by the belief that someone or something is dangerous, likely to cause pain, or a threat; be afraid of (someone or something) as likely to be dangerous, painful, or threatening.

Faith: complete trust or confidence in someone or something; strong belief in God or in the doctrines of a religion, based on spiritual apprehension rather than proof.

What do you fear during your journey? Why?

_____

_____

_____

_____

_____

_____

_____

Are your adapting to someone else's fear based on what someone else has told you? Yes or No

---

"I learned that courage was not the absence of fear, but the triumph over it. The brave man is not he who does not feel afraid, but he who conquers that fear." —Nelson Mandela

---

What will it take for you to replace your fears with faith during your journey?

_____

_____

_____

_____

"Feed your faith and your fear will starve." -Anonymous

You may be asking the question, "How do I feed my faith?" First, you must feed your faith through your spiritual principles.

"Now faith is confidence in what we hope for and assurance about what we do not see."
- Hebrews 11:1

Let me take you back to the bridge. I began to operate in FAITH and not FEAR because one day I knew I would overcome my fear of bridges. It wasn't that I was afraid to go over bridges; I was more concerned with what was under the bridge. Second, you must change your mindset. Think on the positive instead of the negative. Thirdly, change what comes out of your mouth. Begin to speak I can, instead of I can't. Let's start by repeating, "I can complete this journey back to me." "I am worth this journey back to me." "This journey will be worth the trip. "Keep repeating it until you believe it.

Make a list of where you would like to go (ex: college, travel).

_____

_____

_____

_____

_____

As I started my journey in 2018, I knew I did not want to repeat some of the same things as before. For example, I knew I did not want to fight with women when I'm promoting women's empowerment and have launched a nonprofit organization which focuses on women empowerment. I wanted to travel around the world speaking to women who were broken, wanted to be repaired and then eventually fixed so they can live a fulfilling and happy life. Even though this was happening before I started this journey, I wanted to completely walk in my purpose and live the life that I had wanted to live.

What would you like to obtain on this journey back to you?

_____

_____

_____

_____

_____

On this journey, I wanted to obtain joy, happiness and peace. I was tired of living in misery, being sad and in distress.

CHAPTER 6

ACCEPT

_____⌒/⌒_____

Accept: believe or come to recognize, (an opinion, and explanation) as valid or correct.

Throughout this journey, you will have to accept the experience, past and people for who they are. I know it's hard to accept that your children are being rebellious, your marriage didn't work out. You're raising your children alone, to accept no from those that you would say yes to and friends that you thought were your friends, but really weren't. The truth hurts, but as you begin to accept what has happened to you, you can move forward in your journey.

If you don't accept what has happened, you will stay stagnant and continue to dwell on what has happened to you. It's time to be real with yourself. If you must go back to the mirror, please do. It's time to face reality. Accept responsibility for your actions, whether bad or good. Accept the fact that you want to change for the better and you don't want to be at a place that keeps you comfortable and content. Accept the fact that you are worth more than what you've settled for. Accept the fact that there is more to life than what was shown to you from your parents or your environment.

> **"The first step toward change is awareness. The second step is acceptance."**
> **– Nathaniel Branden**

What have you refused to accept during this journey or before? Why?

_____

_____

_____

_____

_____

Ex: Have you not accepted the fact that change is possible and you too can change?

What have you accepted during this journey or before? Why?

_____

_____

_____

_____

_____

_____

_____

Ex: Have you yet accepted the fact that you have changed. Starting this journey allowed you to see that you needed to change and you want better.

Change: *make or become different.*

What steps did you take during your journey to acceptance? Why?

_____

_____

_____

_____

_____

_____

_____

Are there issues, experiences, or things from your past that you can't let go? Why? What steps have you taken to release yourself from your past?

_____

_____

_____

_____

_____

There was a relationship that I could not let go because once again I had made my own plans for my life and didn't plan for the unexpected. A step that I had to take to release myself from my past was to accept things and people for what and who they were. I had to stop living in denial. **Ask yourself, "Is holding on more important than letting go?"**

"Getting over a painful experience is much like crossing monkey bars. You have to let go at some point in order to move forward." -C.S. Lewis

---

CHAPTER 7

FORGIVE

Forgive: stop feeling angry or resentful toward (someone) for an offense, flaw, or mistake.

Who is it that you need to forgive? Why?

_____

_____

_____

_____

_____

If you don't forgive, you will never move forward. You can't stay angry, bitter or mad forever. Yes it hurt, and you may have felt betrayed, but don't miss your blessing living in unforgiveness. You will be stressing and worrying yourself about people and they will be living their best life. Don't you deserve a life that will be filled with happiness, joy, love and peace?

Forgive people and move forward.

"Forgiveness is the remedy. It doesn't mean you are erasing the past or forgetting what happened. It means you're letting go of the resentment and pain, and instead choosing to learn from the incident and move on with your life. Remember, the less time you spend hating the people who hurt you, the more time you'll have to love the people who love you."
-Marc Chernoff

What have you done that God has forgiven you for?

_____

_____

_____

_____

_____

Maybe you can't move forward or forgive others because you haven't forgiven yourself.

What is it that you have not forgiven yourself for?

_____

_____

_____

_____

_____

Before I could move forward, I had to forgive myself for what I allowed. Have you ever said I will never do that, and you find yourself doing the very thing that you said you would never do? If I could be transparent for a moment, I recalled stating that I would never have an abortion. I found myself in the very situation that I said I would never do. I shared with my close friends about my experience after the abortion. I went through having dreams where two little girls would visit me in my sleep for years. I kept wondering why I was having these dreams and why they continued to bother me. In one dream, they would tell me that they were okay, and I would be okay. Then when I found myself doing things that I knew I had no business doing or in relationships with people that were not good for me, they would throw fire at me.

I found myself weeping, twisting and turning and up all night when they would visit me. I had a good friend who would say to me,

"There is therefore no condemnation to them which are in Christ Jesus, because through Christ Jesus the law of the Spirit who gives life has set you free from the law of sin and death."
-Romans 8: 1-3

However, even after being equipped with this Bible verse, I still felt the guilt and shame of having an abortion. It wasn't until I was at an event and I heard a woman share how many abortions she had, that made me release the guilt. She told me I had to release everything and be free. I could no longer carry this. She prayed for me and I felt a burden being lifted. Sometimes you will be sent to a place to hear someone else share their story, to help you understand that you are not the only one and you're not alone. Then it's times you don't know what you can share or who you can share it with because everyone may not have experience what you have experienced.

All advice is not good advice. Not all listening ears are good listeners. As I still continue to deal with my abortion, I had many feelings. I had never been in prison, but I felt as if I was a prisoner in my mind after the abortion and I wanted to be free. I prayed to God, asked Him to forgive me and then I had to forgive myself and be okay with the decision that I made. It was between God and me. I shared this because I am free, and I no longer care about the opinions of others because we all have done things that we were not proud of. For we all have issues and struggles, just because your issue or struggle may not be mine, that you're no different than me. People can judge you. There is only one judge at the end of the day and that is God. Declare that you will no longer be a prisoner. You are free and you will no longer go back to a prison state of mind.

Prison: *a state of confinement or captivity*

Prisoner: *a person who is or feels confined or trapped by a situation or set of circumstances*

Free: *not or no longer confined or imprisoned*

Why do you still feel guilty or ashamed for the things that you've done before or during this journey? Have you not forgiven yourself?

_____

_____

_____

The Journey Back To You

CHAPTER 8

JUDGE WHO

Judge: form an opinion or conclusion about

When I think about the things that I have done, I realize that I was not in a place to judge anyone. We judge people based on what they have done to us or what someone else has shared or experienced with that person. I always judged the women who had affairs with married men due to what I had experienced. I never looked at the root cause of why women involve themselves with married men or why married men could not be faithful to their wife. It was deeper than what I assumed or knew.

I was concerned about my pain and never concerned myself with the pain that the person who caused me the pain had experienced. There is always a root cause as to why people do what they do. Don't assume that the reason is always low self-esteem. Some people repeat what they have seen or what was done to them. Maybe the person may have not had anyone to educate them about self, womanhood or manhood. Even after you've experienced the hurt and pain, it is okay to seek therapy.

I recall seeking therapy only to get out of work for months because I could not handle the stress from home and work. I did not take full advantage of the service being provided to me. I wanted a temporary fix for what I thought was a temporary problem, until I continued to have the problem and found myself back in therapy again. As I found myself back in therapy, this time it was different. I found a place where I could cry, scream and tell it all without being judged. Having someone listen and someone who was concerned about my well-being was what I needed.

This therapist made a difference in my life because she listens, and she didn't tell me what I needed to do because I already knew what I needed to do. Therapy does not label you as crazy. We all need help and an outlet to express how we really feel inside. You don't know what a person may be experiencing and for those of you who may be reading this book and know me, you probably had no idea of some things that I have shared in this book thus far.

Be careful not to judge a person by what they look like because you really don't know their story. I couldn't judge because I am not perfect, and you can't judge because you are not perfect. This is my truth. The journey is about you dealing with your truth and healing so that you can become a better you during and after this journey. Once you heal, forgive and get a better understanding of why people do what they do and understand the reasons behind your judgement, you'll be careful about what you judge and who you judge. Remember what I stated before, "Never say Never" because the very thing that you judge you may find yourself in that situation.

Who was it that you judged? Why?

_____

_____

_____

Why did you judge others? Perhaps you were unaware that you were judging someone.

_____

_____

_____

Was it before you started this journey that you judged someone? Yes or No

How do you feel after you've judged someone?

_____

_____

_____

_____

_____

For the people that you've judged, how can you help them?

_____

_____

_____

_____

_____

As you travel this journey, you will be judged. You will be judged for finally moving forward and no longer staying in situations that caused you to judge others. You may hear the words, "Oh you think you're better now?" It's not that you think you are better, it's I know that I deserve better. Once again, we all will be judged at the end of our lifetime and no one has the right to judge anyone.

Listen before you talk.

Understand before you judge.

The Journey Back To You

CHAPTER 9

HELPING OTHERS

Help: *make it easier for (someone) to do something by offering one's services or resources*

The one thing that I have come to realize is that you can't help and save everyone, when you need help as well. During this journey, you will find those that need your help and those that seek to use you. You will need to understand the difference from being the help or being used. How can you help everyone when you're trying to help yourself during this journey back to you? There will be people that will only concern themselves about their need and what you can do for them. Determine who you will help during this journey so that you won't become frustrated, overwhelmed or stressed. Remember this journey is about you.

Who have you helped during your journey?

_____

_____

_____

_____

_____

Have you sought help from someone before or during your journey? Yes or No

Who have you helped during your journey and was not there for you when you needed them the most? How did you feel?

_____

_____

_____

_____

_____

How will you determine who you will help during your journey moving forward?

_____

_____

_____

_____

I saw a quote that stated, *"You have two hands. One to help yourself, the second to help others."* -Author Unknown

The Journey Back To You

CHAPTER 10

TAKE CARE OF YOURSELF

Self-Care: *the practice of taking an active role in protecting one's own well-being and happiness, during periods of stress.*

I didn't start working on self-care until I realized that it was time for me to start focusing on myself. Self-care is a personal matter. Self-care is for you.

Define self-care. What does it mean to you?

_____

_____

_____

_____

I will share with you below the different aspects to self-care and examples of strategies that I've found useful.

PROFESSIONAL SELF-CARE

Think about activities that help you to be consistent at the level expected of you.

_____

_____

_____

_____

_____

_____

_____

I like to attend professional development trainings to help me find balance with work and my personal life.

What does your workplace offer to help with self-care while at work?

_____

_____

_____

_____

_____

_____

_____

_____

PHYSICAL SELF-CARE

What activities help you to stay fit and healthy?

_____

_____

_____

_____

_____

I still struggle in this area, however, I have obtained a membership at the YMCA. I started going weekly and for some reason I have not been an active member. As a part of your self-care, it is important to make time for exercise throughout your busy day. Often times, you don't even have to go to the gym. You can walk around in the building while you're at work on your lunch break if you're able to. I get lazy too, but I know this is an area that needs improvement. I'm working on aiming for a healthy diet. During this journey, I have worked on a healthy diet so many times and when life hits me, I want a Diet Coke and chocolate.

PSYCHOLOGICAL SELF-CARE

What activities help you to clear your mind?

_____

_____

_____

_____

_____

I find myself writing in my journal to help release what I'm thinking or when I become stressed. There are times when I just need to relax and take a break from everything.

SPIRITUAL SELF-CARE

This involves having a sense of perspective beyond the day-to-day of life.

List what you do for spiritual self-care.

_____

_____

_____

_____

_____

_____

I pray. I attend church on Tuesday's and Sunday's. I listen to inspirational music. I read my Bible. I've learned that my relationship with God is more important than being religious.

RELATIONSHIP SELF-CARE

This is about maintaining healthy and supportive relationships in the community and workplace.

Who do you have healthy relationships with?

_____

_____

_____

_____

_____

How do you define associates and friends?

_____

_____

_____

_____

_____

_____

Do you attend special events with your family and friends? Yes or No If not, Why?

_____

_____

_____

_____

_____

Now it's time to create your own self-care plan using the categories listed above. Complete your self-care plan with activities that you enjoy doing alone or with others. Stick to your plan and practice the activities regularly. As you create your self-care plan, think about what you would do when distractions come. **What will you do to keep focused?**

CHAPTER 11

CONTROL YOUR EMOTIONS

~

Emotions: instinctive or intuitive feeling as distinguished from reasoning or knowledge.

Every time you allow your emotions to dictate your response, you will be completing a self-assessment daily. Most self-assessments are completed because we have reacted off our emotions instead of thinking things through. How many times have you done or said something that you know you should not have? You find yourself apologizing often because you know you were wrong. Ladies be very careful during your time of the month when you know your hormones are wacky. Tell your emotions to line up.

> **"Inner peace begins the moment you choose not to allow another person or event to control your emotions."**
> **–Power Of Positivity**

How do you control your emotions?

_____

_____

_____

_____

_____

Controlling your emotions can be hard at times. What I have learned is I cannot react right away. When reacting right away for me I find myself asking God to forgive me or others. Take a deep breath before reacting to your emotions. Everything that happens in our lives, whether good or bad, serves a bigger purpose. Remember God is in control.

"And we know that for those who love God all things work together for good, for those who are called according to his purpose."
-Romans 8:28

CHAPTER 12

SELF ASSESSMENT

———————～———————

No one can win all the time. But you've got to learn from all you do—both successes and failures. Always do a self-assessment.

Self-Assessment: assessment or evaluation of oneself or one's actions and attitude.

There is always room for self- assessment. Self-assessments are about you, just like this journey is about you. How long will you continue to blame others for the negative responses that you give out to the world? Just like you go to the doctor's when you're not feeling well, every now and then, you may need to complete a self-assessment on yourself when you need to reevaluate some areas in your life.

Why do you think self-assessments are important?

_____

_____

_____

_____

Did you accomplish your goal on your journey that you wanted to obtain in the beginning?

_____

_____

_____

_____

_____

Did you make good choices/ decisions while on your journey?

_____

_____

_____

_____

_____

How can you correct the bad decisions that you may have made on this journey?

_____

_____

_____

_____

_____

How did you communicate to people during this journey?

_____

_____

_____

_____

_____

What are you proud about now that you've completed the beginning of a new journey?

_____

_____

_____

_____

_____

What have you learned on your journey about you?

_____

_____

_____

_____

_____

Did anything or anyone along the way distract you on this journey? If you answered yes, how did you deal with the distractions?

_____

_____

_____

_____

_____

Did you have any temptations on your journey? How did you handle the temptations?

_____

_____

_____

_____

Did you ask for help during this journey? How did you feel after you received your help?

How many times did you have to stop to examine yourself during your journey? What did you have to examine about yourself?

These are some things to think about as you continue your journey. As you begin to deal with you, and be real with you, be prepared for what's to come as you journey back to you. Either you will feed the distractions or people that limited your growth or you will realize that everything or every person does not need a response. The reason why it does not need a response is because you are no longer that person that responds with anger, cursing, fighting, and yelling. Take a deep breath and think about it.

Will it be worth it to lose all your energy and be stressed for something or someone that you could have avoided? These are the questions that I had to ask myself. I failed this test many times and had to re-evaluate myself daily. If you continue to feed the response, you can't grow. This journey is about you and not them or it. How long will you continue to feed that thing or person that is hindering your growth? Your time is valuable.

"Ask yourself if what you're doing today is getting you closer to where you would like to be tomorrow." - Author Unknown

---

CHAPTER 13

CONFIDENCE

Confidence: a feeling of self-assurance arising from one's appreciation of one's own abilities or qualities.

Have you struggled with low confidence or low self-esteem? Yes or No

People with low self-esteem are more likely to sabotage themselves when something good happens to them because they don't feel deserving. - Author Unknown

Some examples of low confidence/low self-esteem may be shame, blame, putting other's down, poor self- image, lack of boundaries, withdrawn and negative.

What areas did you have low self-esteem in?

_____

_____

_____

_____

_____

What did you do to build your self-esteem?

_____

_____

_____

_____

_____

Below are examples of ways that may help you to build your self-esteem.

Start changing how you see and speak to yourself. Instead of waiting for someone to tell you how beautiful you are, tell yourself that you are beautiful. Stop comparing yourself to others.

> **"Don't compare yourself to others. You have no idea what their journey is all about." -Author Unknown**

Practice being the best version of you. There are no perfect people in the world. Accept your flaws. Everyone makes mistakes. Don't be so hard on yourself. Focus on what you can control and that's you. Do what makes you happy, this is your life. Celebrate you every chance that you get. Help those that are worthy of your help and not those that use you. You are the help and it feels good to help those that appreciate you. Surround yourself with people that will encourage, empower, motivate, pray and support you to feel better about yourself. Avoid those individuals who bring negativity to your life.

Lastly, walk in a room like you own it with your head held high with a smile on your face and don't be worried about who's in the room. You now have begun to build your confidence.

> **"You gain strength, courage, and confidence by every experience in which you really stop to look fear in the face. You must do the thing which you think you cannot do."**
> **-Eleanor Roosevelt**

When you look at me, don't think for a moment that I was always confident. I had to build myself back up daily.

> **"Confidence is preparation. Everything else is beyond your control." - Richard Kline**

I struggle with my self-esteem as I got older because I compared myself to other women due to what I was experiencing in my relationship at the time. However, once I came back to reality and began **re-examining**, **re-evaluating** and **reinventing** myself. I had no time to compare myself with other women. I started looking in the mirror and speaking to myself. I started with I am beautiful and my color or size didn't matter. I was starting to understand my worth as a woman after losing myself.

"Every woman that finally figured out her worth has picked up her suitcases of pride and boarded a flight to freedom, which landed in the valley of change."
-Shannon L. Alder

CHAPTER 14

RE-EXAMINE, RE-EVALUATE & RE-INVENT

Re-examine: to examine (someone or something) again especially from a different point of view

As I look back over my life, I was very comfortable in my situations. The thought of change sounded impossible. Change sounded impossible because I didn't understand or realize that change was possible.

> **"Progress is impossible without change, and those who cannot change their minds cannot change anything." -George Bernard Shaw**

If I didn't make some changes in my life, I probably would still be stuck and unhappy. I had to re-examine where I was in my life and where I wanted to go.

> **"You must make a choice to take a chance or your life will never change." -Anonymous**

What areas in your life need to be re-examined? Why? (Ex: job, finances, friendships, relationships)

_____

_____

_____

_____

_____

Re-evaluate: to evaluate (something or someone) again especially with regard to changes or new information

Even after you have examined yourself, there may come a time where you may need to re-evaluate yourself over and over again. For example, I had to evaluate my attitude and tone daily. Even though I knew there will be challenges daily, I don't want my attitude and tone affecting my life personally or professionally. There were times that I had to apologize to people for my attitude and tone. Sometimes it's not what you say, but how you say it. As the challenges arise I began to have self-talks with myself before responding. I realized that every response did not deserve a reaction. By changing my attitude there were certain people who responded to me different, because the old way no longer worked for the new person. I learned this as I matured and began re-evaluating myself.

What are areas in your life that you find yourself re-evaluating?

_____

_____

_____

_____

_____

"Attitude is a choice. Happiness is a choice. Optimism is a choice. Kindness is a choice. Giving is a choice. Respect is a choice. Whatever choice you make, makes you. Choose wisely." -Roy T Bennett

Re-inventing: to remake or redo completely

As you focus on change and your future, you'll be surprised of what you can accomplish. I envisioned a future that was better than my past. Now that I know who I am, it was time to reinvent myself. I no longer wanted to be Kisha. Kisha had experienced the bad and the good throughout her life. I could not take Kisha into my new. I had to give up the old to give birth to the new. However, I wanted to be who I was created to be and that was Lakisha Inspires and Women Of Courage. It was time for a makeover.

> **"Your power to choose your direction of your life allows you to reinvent yourself, to change your future, and to powerfully influence the rest of creation." -Stephen Covey**

Who I was in the past, or who I was in the present, was not dictating who I wanted to be tomorrow or in the future. I was once broken, wanted to be repaired. Today I am fixed. I am beautiful. I am strong. I empower. I inspire. I am bold and confident.

> **"Every day, you reinvent yourself. You're always in motion. But you decide every day: forward or backward." -James Altucher**

Why reinvent yourself?

_____

_____

_____

_____

_____

Do you think it will be difficult for you to reinvent yourself and if so, Why?

_____

_____

_____

_____

_____

The Journey Back To You

CHAPTER 15

ENCOURAGE YOURSELF

Encourage: to inspire with courage, spirit, or hope; to attempt to persuade; give support, confidence, or hope to (someone); give support and advice to (someone) so that they will do or continue to do something.

Sometimes you will have to encourage yourself. There may be days that no one will be available to answer your phone calls. You will have to learn how to encourage yourself. There may be times when you feel lonely` and all alone. You will have to encourage yourself. There may be times that you experience no one cheering for you. You will have to encourage yourself. There may be times that you receive no recognition for all the good work that you do. You will have to encourage yourself.

How do you encourage yourself?

_____

_____

_____

_____

_____

_____

_____

_____

How do you encourage others?

_____

_____

_____

_____

_____

_____

_____

_____

_____

CHAPTER 16

LOVE YOURSELF

Love: *an intense feeling of deep affection; a great interest and pleasure in something; feel a deep romantic or sexual attachment to (someone).*

It's very easy to say the words, "I love me." Do you love yourself? Yes or No

Define love in your own words.

_____

_____

_____

_____

_____

_____

_____

Have you ever loved someone more than you have loved yourself? Yes or No

Why do you think you loved others more than you loved yourself if you answered yes?

_____

_____

_____

_____

_____

How do you love yourself?

_____

_____

_____

_____

_____

"If I was to define love I would say: Love is patient. Love is kind. Love does not envy. Love does not boast. Love is not proud. Love is not rude. Love always trusts. Love always hopes. Love never fails." –1 Corinthians 13: 4-7

I was accustomed to love that hurt. Love should have never had to hurt. When I was young, I didn't have a clear understanding of what love was. I loved people more than I loved myself. I would put people's feelings before my very own.

> **"Your relationship with yourself sets the tone for every other relationship you have." –Author Unknown**

Today, I had to grow into my relationship with God and know that He loved me more than anyone. God's love for me was everlasting. I had to start caring for myself just like I cared for everyone else. I had to be okay with people calling me selfish. However, it wasn't selfish when I was caring and loving everyone else, but myself. I had to set boundaries and concern myself with those things that were important to me. Lastly, I had to do what I needed to do for myself.

> **"Loving yourself starts with liking yourself, which starts with respecting yourself, which starts with thinking of yourself in positive ways." -Author Unknown**

You have made it to your destination. Even if you had to travel this road by yourself, it is okay. No one can travel the road for you. There were things that you needed to understand about you as you went along your journey. You may have thought that you would not complete this journey, but know that it was within your reach. This journey was worth the trip back to you!

> **"Sometimes it's the journey that teaches you a lot about your destination." -Drake**

Lakisha Selby, born and raised in Wilmington, Delaware is a mother of four who has personally faced many challenges. As a woman that has experienced trials and tribulations that could have very-well defeated her; she persevered. What did not kill her has made her stronger. She re-emerged determined to turn her pain into purpose. She seeks to empower and to help women she has encountered who could relate to and who needed to hear a positive word by being transparent and sharing her story. Not only has Lakisha's personal experiences contributed to the birthing of Women Of Courage, but also working in a local women's shelter in Wilmington, Delaware, has inadvertently given her the opportunity to see, firsthand the common conditions and circumstances that derail women and leave them off track emotionally and financially.

In 2012, Lakisha held her 1st Annual Women of Courage Chat & Chew. More than a hundred women from all walks of life were in attendance for this inaugural event. The feedback was tremendous with the consensus being that it succeeded in making women feel uplifted, empowered, inspired and motivated. The speakers, many of whom shared not only encouraging words, but real-life stories of struggle and triumph were particularly effective.

Lakisha continues to strive and conquer new accolades. In May of 2013 she received her Bachelor of Science Degree from Springfield College of Human Services in Wilmington, Delaware Campus. She continued her educational journey shortly after, earning her Master's Degree in Administration Of Human Service from Wilmington University. Lakisha Selby has overcome many obstacles that have helped her grow to a point of self-empowerment and self-love that she feels driven and inspired to share. She has made it her spiritual obligation and life's mission to pay it forward by helping other women build their self-esteem, personal development and find the empowerment within them to reach their full potential. Armed with this information, she continues to develop an ever-growing understanding of the needs and sensibilities of women, overall to infuse into her organization and its mission.

Book me to speak at your next event!

Send an email to:

lakishainspires@gmail.com

Learn more about Lakisha at: www.lakishainspires.com

www.ingramcontent.com/pod-product-compliance
Lightning Source LLC
Chambersburg PA
CBHW072207090426
42740CB00012B/2422